Great lines from country songs so you can talk real purty while you're
flirtin'
                    lovin'
                                      cheatin'
                leavin'
drinkin'
                weepin'
                          honky tonkin'
            and just gettin' by

How to Talk Country

Collected by Doug Todd
Illustrated by Richard Anderson

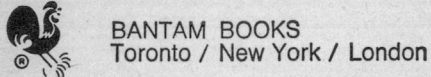
BANTAM BOOKS
Toronto / New York / London

HOW TO TALK COUNTRY
A Bantam Book / August 1980

Book designed by Cathy Marinaccio
Illustrations by Richard Anderson.
All rights reserved.
Copyright © 1980 by Doug Todd.
Illustrations copyright © 1980 by Bantam Books, Inc.
Cover art copyright © 1980 by Bantam Books, Inc.
This book may not be reproduced in whole or in part, by mimeograph or any other means, without permission.
For information address: Bantam Books, Inc.

ISBN 0-553-14346-8

Published simultaneously in the United States and Canada

Bantam Books are published by Bantam Books, Inc. Its trademark, consisting of the words "Bantam Books" and the portrayal of a bantam, is Registered in U.S. Patent and Trademark Office and in other countries. Marca Registrada. Bantam Books, Inc., 666 Fifth Avenue, New York, New York 10103.

PRINTED IN THE UNITED STATES OF AMERICA

0 9 8 7 6 5 4 3 2 1

I want to live fast,
love hard, die young
and leave a beautiful memory.

Introduction

If anybody should know how to talk country, it's me. Where I went to high school, in Lewisville, Texas, our football team's nickname is the Fightin' Farmers. Then I went to Oklahoma State, which is the Cowboys. Then I played nine years for Dallas, which is also the Cowboys. I was also a rodeo cowboy until I broke my knee. And now I work for the U.S. Tobacco Co., which makes snuff, which is used by cowboys and others.

So I ought to know how to talk country.

I want to warn you, though, that this book won't really teach you how to talk country. You probably want it to, but it won't.

What the book will do, if you don't already talk country, is make you appreciate people who do. It will make you a basically better person, and will improve your relationships in all walks of life. It will make you the envy of your friends, and you'll have more of them after you digest all this knowledge.

What I'm trying to say, is, this book ain't bad if you ain't used to much.

—Walt Garrison

Honky-Tonkin'

Honky Tonk Angel

It wasn't God that made honky-tonk angels.

Red hot memories, ice cold beer.

Her scepter is a wine glass, and this bar stool is her throne.

Gonna honky-tonk right out on you.

Pick me up on the way down.

I love everything in nylons, every place with neon.

Thanks to the cathouse I'm in the doghouse with you.

All the good timin' ladies will drive a man crazy, I'll spend my whole paycheck right here.

If I'm gonna sink (might as well go to the bottom).

I'm the only hell Mama ever raised.

It's a naked on the back porch Saturday night.

It just dawned on me what sundown does to you.

I've been honky-tonkin' too long.

Flirtin'

Heaven's just a sin away.

She never met a man she didn't like.

Help me make it through the night.

You're candy in the window of my mind.

I'd love to lay you down.

We're not exactly strangers. I've already loved you in my mind.

Playin' hard to get is gettin' hard to play.

Make up your mind or I'll lose mine.

Your sweet lies just turned down my sheets again.

If you'll be my tall dark stranger, I'll be your San Antone rose.

Cheatin'

*If fingerprints showed up on skin,
wonder whose I'd find on you?*

You'd make an angel want to cheat.

*Baby you're something, but she's
everything.*

*It's bad when you're caught with the
goods.*

While I'm putting on my makeup, I'm putting on the one that really loves me.

When you're undercover lovers, you lay low.

It meant goodbye to me when you said hello to him.

I don't want no stranger sleeping in my bed.

She's everybody's woman, I'm nobody's man.

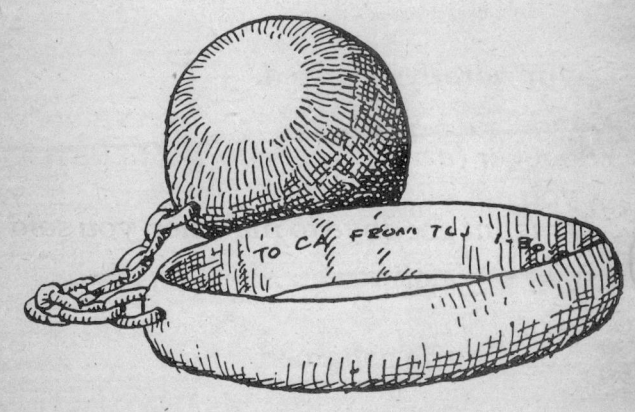

Does my ring hurt your finger when you go out at night?

It's all wrong but it's alright.

Layin' here, lyin' in bed.

Whoever turned you on forgot to turn you off.

Lovin' on back streets, livin' on Main.

We oughta be ashamed.

Liars 1, Believers 0.

It was always so easy to find an unhappy woman 'til I started looking for mine.

Hell yes, I cheated, and I'll do it again.

Country Lovin'

He's a rared back, belly rubbin', toe stomping country lovin' lover.

You're gonna love yourself in the morning because I'm gonna love you all night long.

I couldn't be me without you.

While I was reaching for her body she was reaching for my soul.

I've got the hungries for your love, and I'm waiting in your welfare line.

My good girl treats me bad, but my bad girl treats me good.

Old flames can't hold a candle to you.

Nothing sure looked good on you.

I'd rather be in Tucson with Rosa dancin' real slow and kissing on her neck.

I've got the all overs for you all over me.

She's just too good to be true, but she is.

Let's call it a day and get on with the night.

I'd rather die young than grow old without you.

You decorated my life.

Somewhere between lust and sitting home watching TV.

Bad Lovin'

You must think my bed's a bus stop
the way you come and go.

Love can't make it when we're sleeping back to back.

We called it magic, then we called it tragic, and finally we called it quits.

When do we stop starting all over again?

A woman can't help the way that she feels when the tingle becomes a chill.

Living together alone.

I'd love to live with you again, but then I couldn't live with me.

It's not love but it's not bad.

Just makin' love don't make it love.

What's a nice girl like you doing in a love like this?

I love you, I just don't like you.

This time I've hurt her more than she loves me.

You changed everything about me but my name.

I haven't seen you with the lights on for two nights in a row.

Your negligee has turned to flannel nightgowns.

We can't build a fire in the rain.

The chances of you ever changing are as slim as your two loving arms.

Somehow it seems the best in you brings out the worst in me.

Home is where I hang my head.

Losin'

Flushed from the bathroom of your heart.

Don't it make my brown eyes blue.

I need somebody bad tonight 'cause I just lost somebody good.

The Devil ain't a lonely woman's friend.

There's nothing cold as ashes, after the fire is gone.

The bridge washed out, I can't swim, and my baby's on the other side.

That girl who waits on tables used to wait for me at home.

*When I came here, I brought my pride,
    but just like you it's gone.*

*He's walking in my tracks, but he can't
    fill my shoes.*

Nothing takes the place of you.

The bitter they are, the harder they fall.

*I have loved some ladies, and I have
    loved Jim Beam, and they both tried
    to kill me in 1973.*

You're driving me out of your mind.

Today I started loving you again.

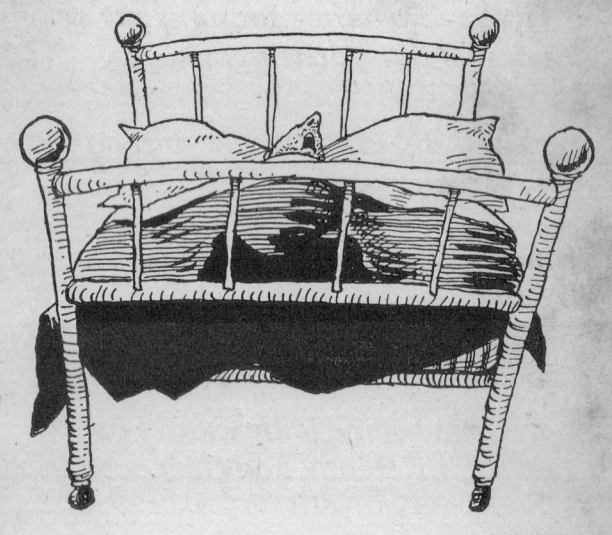

Livin' single in a double bed.

So I'll just wait for her, looking out my window through the pain.

What's the use to try to get over you? I've still got you all over me.

Her daddy likes guns and he don't like me.

Just like the dawn, my heart is silently breaking.

Honey, all your get-up-and-go done got up and went.

The only thing I can count on now is my fingers.

Oh where is my enchanted prince?
I hope I find him soon
It seems I've kissed a hundred frogs,
Some apes and one baboon.

Wailin'

Even cowgirls get the blues.

A working man can't get nowhere today.

My uncle used to love me but she died.

Too late to worry, too blue to cry.

It takes me all night long to do what I used to do all night long.

I ain't got no business doing business today.

I'm back at the bottom with no will to climb.

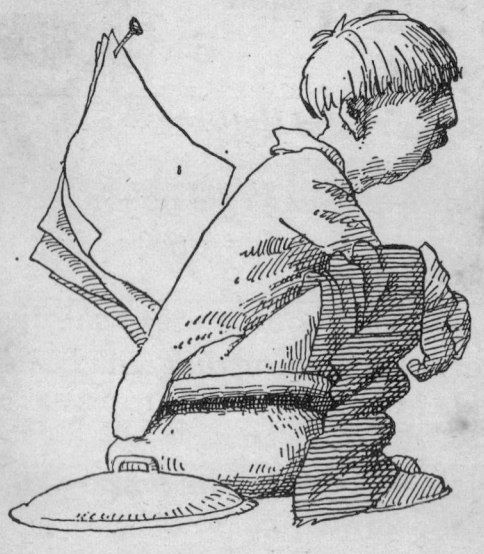

I can still hear the music in the restroom, but they can't see the hurt on my face.

Hey Barnum and Bailey, can you use one more clown?

Lord it's hard to be an outlaw when you're a millionaire.

I've never had a thing that ain't been used.

I keep lookin' for tomorrow and findin' yesterdays.

All the gold in California is in a bank in the middle of Beverly Hills in somebody else's name.

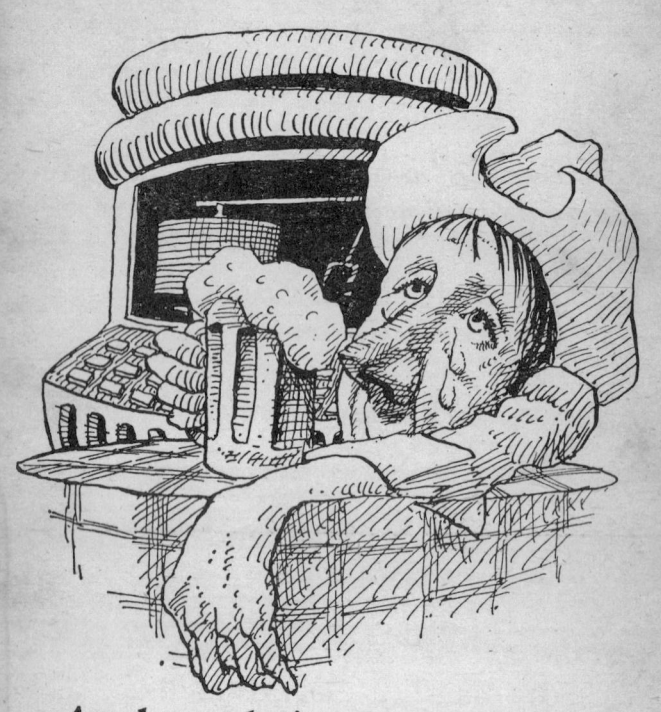

A sad song don't care whose heart it breaks.

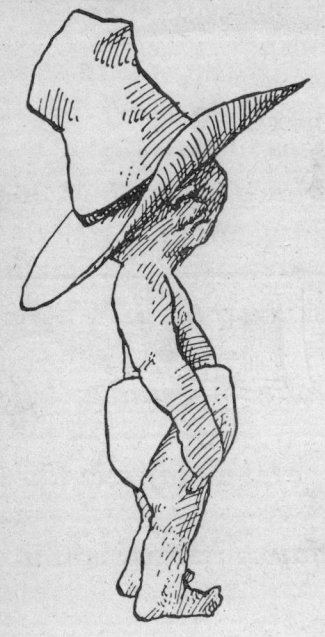

Mommas, don't let your babies grow up to be cowboys.

Them that ain't got can't lose.

Pride's not hard to swallow, once you chew it long enough.

I'm always on a mountain when I fall.

I'd walk a mile for a smile.

All the beer and all my friends are gone.

Should I come home or should I go crazy?

Drinkin'

The alcohol of fame.

The power of positive drinking.

I skipped work last Friday to drink this month's rent.

I'll be under the table when I get over you.

Heaven was a drink of wine.

Tonight my solitaire turns into gin.

Let me go home whiskey.

She's acting single, I'm drinking doubles.

It's the bottle against the Bible in the battle for Daddy's soul.

From the bottle to the bottom, stool by stool.

Four in the floor, and a fifth beneath the seat.

You took my friends and you took me too, whiskey I gave it all to you.

Leavin'

She caught me lying and then she caught a train.

*If practice makes perfect, I'm leaving
   you perfect this time.*

*I've been a long time leaving, but I'll be
   a long time gone.*

She even woke me up to say goodbye.

*Thank God and Greyhound you're
   gone.*

*Sayin' you're leavin's so much easier
   than leavin' and sayin' goodbye.*

*When you leave Amarillo, turn out
   the lights.*

Her women's intuition must have told her I was into wishin' I could leave.

Why have you left the one you left me for?

Let's say goodbye like we said hello (in a friendly kind of way).

Next to me my soon to be the one I left behind.

When I stop leaving I'll be gone.

Lay back down and love me, and leave the leaving for later on.

Fightin'

She don't get mad, she just gets even.

Don't tell me you're sorry, 'cause I know how sorry you are.

Every time you throw some dirt, you lose a little ground.

You can't make a heel toe the mark.

Just pass me by if you're only passing through.

I don't want to play house.

How come my dog don't bark when you come around?

*You better close your face and stay
   outa my way if you don't wanta go
   to Fist City.*

*Don't come home a-drinkin' with
   lovin' on your mind.*

You can have her.

*Big ain't always judged by just how
   tall you stand.*

Look what the dog drug in.

*That little sucker crawled all up and
   down each side of me.*

Let's shake hands and come out lovin'.

Gettin' By

I take a lot of pride in what I am.

The work we done was hard. At night we'd sleep 'cause we were tired.

My heroes have always been cowboys.

*Some folks call me lazy,
A good for nothin' jerk
But I've got my wife a real good job
So I don't have to work.*

The older the violin, the sweeter the music.

I'm a genuine Texas good guy.

The school of hard knocks, it never gave me no diploma.

The undertaker's gonna have
   a hard time
Wipin' this smile off a my lips,
'Cause livin' to me is to be carefree,
Just a-singin' and a-shakin' my hips.

*Long live the red neck and the good
   times from a can.*
*Long live white socks and the ordinary
   man.*

Never's just the echo of forever.

*Yesterday's dead and tomorrow is
   blind. I live one day at a time.*

*Faster horses, younger women, older
   whiskey, more money.*

*Drop kick me, Jesus, through the goal
   posts of life.*

*If I'da known that I was gonna live this
   long, I'da taken better care of myself.*

Proud To Keep It Country

*Well, I'm proud to keep it country
No one can take it from me
All the pickers and the grinners and the country singers
Well, they're all friends of mine*

*Oh, I'm proud to keep it country
It's the only music for me
All those hand-clapping, knee-slapping, true-life stories
That have all been set to rhyme*

*Well, now years ago I wandered looking for the answer
I saw the world from different points of view
The rockers they tried to roll me, but they could not console me
So country I'm coming back to you.*

Credits
How To Talk Country

These are the titles of the songs from which the individual lines in this book are drawn, along with the wonderful writers who made each of them possible. The credits follow the order of the lines as they appear on each page of the book.

We thank all of the writers and their publishers for their contributions to HOW TO TALK COUNTRY.

PAGE V

"Live Fast, Love Hard, Die Young"
Joe Allison
© 1954 Central Songs, Inc.
Used by permission; all rights reserved

PAGE 2

"It Wasn't God That Made Honky-Tonk Angels"
J.D. Miller
Peer International

"Red Hot Memories, Ice Cold Beer"
Tom T. Hall
Hallnote Music

"Queen of the Silver Dollar"
Words and music by Shel Silverstein
© 1972 Evil Eye Music, Inc., New York, N.Y.
Used by permission; all rights reserved

"Gonna Honky-Tonk Right Out On You"
Harlan Howard
Baray Music, Inc.

"Pick Me Up On The Way Down"
Harlan Howard
Tree Publishing Co., Inc.

"Neons and Nylons"
G. Sutton, R. Steagall
Rodeo Cowboy Music, Inc., & Otter Creek Music

"Thanks to the Cathouse (I'm in the Doghouse With You)"
Max Barnes, Jim Valenti, Frank Saulino
Screen Gems-EMI Music & Colgem-EMI Music, Inc.

PAGE 3

"I Remember While Drinkin' In Texas"
Don King, Dave Woodward
Wiljex Publishing Co.

"If I'm Gonna Sink (Might As Well Go to the Bottom)"
Johnny Paycheck, A. Mayhew
Mayhew Music

"I'm The Only Hell Mama Ever Raised"
Mack Vickery, Wayne Kemp, Bobby Brochers
Tree Publishing Co., Inc.

"Naked On The Back Porch"
Don King & Dave Woodward
Wiljex Publishing Co.

"It Just Dawned On Me What Sundown Does To You"
Porter Wagoner
Owepar Publishing

"I've Been Honky-Tonkin' Too Long"
William Collins, Dickie Lee
Hall-Clements Publications

PAGE 4

"Heaven's Just A Sin Away"
J. Gillespie
Lorville Music Co.

"She Never Met A Man"
Dolly Parton
© International copyright secured 1969 Velvet Apple Music
Used by permission; all rights reserved

"Help Me Make It Through The Night"
Kris Kristofferson
Combine Music Corp.

"Candy In The Window"
Tom T. Hall
Hallnote Music

"I'd Love To Lay You Down"
Johnny MacRae
Music City Music, Inc.

PAGE 5

"I've Already Loved You In My Mind"
Conway Twitty
© 1977 Twitty Bird Music Publishing Co.

PAGE 6

"Playin' Hard To Get"
John Thompson
Bobby Goldsboro Music, Inc.

"Should I Come Home Or Should I Go Crazy"
Joe Allen
© 1973 Tree Publishing Co., Inc.

"Your Sweet Lies Just Turned Down My Sheets Again"
James Vest, David Chamberlain
Continental Enterprises

"I'll Be Your San Antone Rose"
Susanna Clark
© 1975 World Song Publishing, Inc.
Used by permission; all rights reserved

PAGE 7

"If Fingerprints Showed Up On Skin"
Written by Freddie Hart, Kenneth E. Hunt
© 1976, 1970 Blue Book Music, Bakersfield, California and Ching-Ring Music, Inc., Nashville, Tennessee

"You'd Make An Angel Want To Cheat"
James Zerface, Robert Morrison, William Zerface
Combine Music Corp. and Southern Nights Music

"Baby You're Something, But She's Everything"
Claude Putnam, Don Hook, R. Vanhoy
Cross Key Publishing Co., Inc. & Tree Publishing Co., Inc.

"It's Bad When You're Caught With The Goods"
Tommy Overstreet, Dale Vest
Duchess Music Corp. and Tommy Overstreet Music

PAGE 8

"Midnight Oil"
Joe Allen
© 1973 Tree Publishing Co., Inc.

"Undercover Lovers"
Even Stevens, Sherry Grooms
Deb-Dave Music, Inc.

"It Meant Goodbye To Me When You Said Hello To Him"
Lefty Frizzell, Abe Mulkey
Al Gallico Music Corp.

"I Don't Want No Stranger Sleeping In My Bed"
Wild Bill Emerson, George Jones
Uncanny Music and Cypress Music, Inc.

"She's Everybody's Woman, I'm Nobody's Man"
Sanger D. Shafer, Moe Bandy
Acuff-Rose Publications, Inc.
All rights reserved

PAGE 9

"Does My Ring Hurt Your Finger"
Don Robertson, John Crutchfield, Doris Clement
Jando Music Inc. and Don Robertson Music Corp.

PAGE 10

"It's All Wrong But It's Alright"
Giorgio Moroder, Pete Bellotte
Rick's Music, Inc.

"Layin' Here, Lyin' In Bed"
Bobby Bare, Billy Shaver
ATV Music

"Whoever Turned You On Forgot To Turn You Off"
David Wilkins, Timothy Marshall
Emerald Isle Music and Battleground Music

"Lovin' On Back Streets"
Hugh King
Contention Music

"We Oughta Be Ashamed"
Earl Montgomery, George Jones
Uncanny Music

"Liars 1, Believers Zero"
Glenn Martin
Tree Publishing Co., Inc.

"'Til I Started Looking For Mine"
Sanger D. Shafer, A.L. "Doodle" Owens
© 1974 Acuff-Rose Publications, Inc. and Hill and Range Songs, Inc.
Used by permission; all rights reserved

"Hell Yes, I Cheated"
Royce Sutton, Larry Cheshier
Flagship Music

PAGE 11

"Country Lovin' Lover"
Fran Powers
Con Brio Music

PAGE 12

"You're Gonna Love Yourself In The Morning"
Donald Fritts
Combine Music Corp.

"I Couldn't Be Me Without You"
Billy Jo Shaver
ATV Music Corp.

"A Different Kind of Flower"
Gary Sefton
Open Road Music, Inc. 75% & Memory Music Co. 25%

"Waitin' In Your Welfare Line"
Written by Buck Owens, Don Rich and Nat Stuckey
© 1966, 1971 Blue Book Music, Bakersfield, California

"Your Good Girl's Gonna Go Bad"
Billy Sherrill, Glenn Sutton
© 1967 Al Gallico Music Corp.

"Old Flames Can't Hold A Candle To You"
Hugh Moffatt, Pebe Sebert
Rightsong, Music, Inc.

PAGE 13
"Nothing Sure Looked Good On You"
Jim Rushing
Coal Miners Music, Inc.

PAGE 14
"Pretty Rosa"
Michael Lorenz
Wiljex Publishing Co.

"I've Got The AllOvers For You All Over Me"
Freddie Hart
Blue Book Music

"She's Too Good To Be True"
Johnny Duncan
Pi-Gem Music Publishers, Inc.
Used by permission; all rights reserved

"Let's Call It A Day And Get On With The Night"
Dave Burgess, Don Pfrimmer
Singletree Music

"I'd Rather Die Young (Than Grow Old Without You)"
Beasley Smith, Billy Vaughn, Randy Wood
© 1953 Milene Music, Inc.
Used by permission; all rights reserved

"You Decorated My Life"
Robert Morrison, Debby Hupp
Music City Music, Inc.

"Between Lust And Watching TV"
Bill Anderson
© 1974 Stallion Music Inc.

PAGE 15
"Standing Room Only"
Charles Silvers, Susan Manchester
© 1975 World Song Publishing, Inc.
Used by permission; all rights reserved

PAGE 16
"Sleeping Single In A Double Bed"
Kye Fleming, Dennis Morgan
Pi-Gem Music Publishers, Inc.
Used by permission; all rights reserved

"Quits"
Danny O'Keefe
© 1975 Warner Tamerlane Publishing Corp. & Road Canon Music Inc. All rights Res. Used by permission.

"When Do We Stop Starting All Over Again"
Mark Forbus
Alamo Village Music

"When The Tingle Becomes A Chill"
Lola Dillon; Howard Harlan
© 1973 Tree Publishing Co., Inc./Harlan Howard Songs

"Living Together Alone"
Albert Lynch
Delton Music Publishing

"I'd Love To Live With You Again"
Dick Overbey
© 1967 Back Bay Music and Court of Kings

PAGE 17
"It's Not Love But It's Not Bad"
Glenn Martin, Hank Cochran
Tree Publishing Co., Inc.

PAGE 18
"Just Makin' Love Don't Make It Love"
Johnny Paycheck
Algee Music Corp.

"What's A Nice Girl Like You (Doing In A Love Like This)?"
Kenny Walker
Acuff-Rose Publications, Inc.

"I Love You, I Just Don't Like You"
Freddie Hart
Hartline Music

"This Time I've Hurt Her More Than She Loves Me"
Earl Conley, Mark Larkin
Blue Moon Music

"You Changed Everything About Me But My Name"
Hank Cochran, Jeannie Seely
© 1967 Tree Publishing Co., Inc.

"Standing Room Only"
Charles Silvers, Susan Manchester
© 1975 World Song Publishing Inc.
Used by permission; all rights reserved

PAGE 19

"Honey, All Your Get-Up-And-Go Done Got Up And Went"
Kendal Franceschi
Concorde Publishing Co.

"We Can't Build A Fire In The Rain"
Bud Reneau
Chess Music Inc.

"I'm Turning Off A Memory"
Merle Haggard
Shade Tree Music

"No One Feels My Hurt The Way You Do"
Hillman Hall
Hallnote Music

"Home Is Where I Hang My Head"
Harlan Howard
Tree Publishing Co., Inc.

PAGE 20

"Flushed From The Bathroom Of Your Heart"
Jack Clement
Jack Music Inc.

"Don't It Make My Brown Eyes Blue"
Richard Leigh
United Artists Music Co., Inc.

"I Need Somebody Bad"
Ben Peters
Ben Peters Music

"The Devil Ain't A Lonely Woman's Friend"
Dallas Frazier, Sanger D. Shafer
Acuff-Rose Publications, Inc.

"After The Fire Is Gone"
L.E. White
© 1969 Twitty Bird Music Publishing Co.

"The Bridge Washed Out"
Jimmy Louis, Sandra Smith, Marty Melschee
Brim Music Inc.

"That Girl Who Waits On Tables Used To Wait For Me At Home"
Bobby P. Barker
Chess Music Inc.

PAGE 21

"Here I Am In Dallas, Where The Hell Are You?"
Ronny Hughes, Terry Ishmael, Lamar Morris
Bocephus Music, Inc.

"He Can't Fill My Shoes"
Larry Kingston, Frank Dycus
© 1974 Window Music Publishing Co., Inc.
Used by permission; all rights reserved

"Nothing Takes The Place Of You"
Patrick Robinson, Touissant McCall
Suma Music Publishing

"The Bitter They Are, The Harder They Fall"
Larry Gatlin
First Generation Music Co.

"Family Tradition"
Hank Williams, Jr.
Bocephus Music, Inc.

"You're Driving Me Out Of You"
Johnny Koonse
Chess Music Inc.
Used by permission; all rights reserved

"Today I Started Loving You Again"
Merle Haggard, Bonny Owens
Blue Book Music

PAGE 22

"Livin' Single In A Double Bed"
Glenn Martin
Tree Publishing Co., Inc.

PAGE 23

"Looking Out My Window Through The Pain"
John Schweers
Chess Music Inc.
Used by permission; all rights reserved

"All Over Me"
Ben Peters
Ben Peters Music and Charsy Music

"Pretty Rosa"
Michael Lorenz
Wiljex Publishing Co.

"She Even Woke Me Up To Say Goodbye"
By Mickey Newbury and Douglas Gilmore
© 1969 Acuff-Rose Publications, Inc.
Used by permission; all rights reserved

"Honey, All Your Get-Up-And-Go Done Got Up And Went"
Kendal Franceschi
Concorde Publishing Co.

"(My Friends Are Gonna Be) Strangers"
Liz Anderson
© 1964 Fred Rose Music, Inc.
Used by permission; all rights reserved

PAGE 24

"How Many Frogs Do I Have To Kiss?"
Frank McPherson/Marlin Lewis
Wiljex Publishing Co.

PAGE 25

"Even Cowgirls Get The Blues"
Rodney Crowell
© 1977-Visa Music

"A Working Man Can't Get Nowhere Today"
Merle Haggard
Shade Tree Music, Inc.

"My Uncle Used To Love Me But She Died"
Roger Miller
Tree Publishing Co., Inc.

"Too Late To Worry, Too Blue To Cry"
Al Dexter
Unichappell Music Inc., Al Dexter Songs, and Elvis Presley Music

"It Takes Me All Night Long"
Gary Stewart, Bill Eldridge
Forrest Hills Music, Inc.

"I Ain't Got No Business Doing Business Today"
Johnny Slate, William Morrison
House of Gold Music, Inc. and Tree Publishing Co., Inc.

"Backside of 30"
John Conlee
House of Gold Music, Inc. and Pommard Music Co.

PAGE 26

"I Can Still Hear The Music In The Restroom"
Tom T. Hall
Hallnote Music

PAGE 27

"Hey Barnum and Bailey"
Charles Stewart, K.W. Hagler, Jerry Abbott
Pantego Sound

"Hard To Be An Outlaw"
Jim Aho
Con Brio Music

"I've Never Had A Thing That Ain't Been Used"
Johnny Rodriquez
Hallnote Music

"Lookin' For Tomorrow (And Findin' Yesterdays)"
Billy Arr, Billy Allds
Sawgrass Music Publishers, Inc.

"All The Gold In California"
Larry Gatlin
Larry Gatlin Music

PAGE 28

"A Sad Song Don't Care Whose Heart It Breaks"
Tom T. Hall
Hallnote Music

PAGE 29

"Mommas, Don't Let Your Babies Grow Up To Be Cowboys"
Ed Bruce, Patsy Bruce
© 1975 Tree Publishing Co., Inc. & Sugarplum Music Co.

PAGE 30

"Them That Ain't Got Can't Lose"
Nelly Smith
Painted Desert Music

"Pride's Not Hard To Swallow"
Jerry Chesnut
Passkey Music, Inc.

"I'm Always On A Mountain When I Fall"
Chuck Howard
Shade Tree Music Inc. & ATV Music Corp.

"I'd Walk A Mile For A Smile"
Billy Deaton & Clyde Pitts
Con Brio Music

"All The Beer And All My Friends Are Gone"
Bill Anderson, Mary Turner
Stallion Music, Inc.

"Should I Come Home Or Should I Go Crazy"
Joe Allen
© 1973 Tree Publishing Co., Inc.

PAGE 31

"The Alcohol Of Fame"
Gary Sargeants
Hallnote Music

PAGE 32

"The Power Of Positive Drinking"
Rick Klang, Don Pfrimmer
Singletree Music

"Backside of 30"
John Conlee
House of Gold Music, Inc. & Pommard Music Co.

"Under The Table"
Tom T. Hall, Hillman Hall
© 1968 by Newkeys Music, Inc.
Copyright Assigned to Unichappel Music, Inc.
International Copyright Secured
Used by permission; all rights reserved

"Heaven Was A Drink Of Wine"
Sanger D. Shafer
Acuff-Rose Publications Inc.

"Tonight My Solitaire Turns Into Gin"
Sterling Whipple
Tree Publishing Co., Inc.

PAGE 33

"Let Me Go Home Whiskey"
Henri Shifts
Unart Music Corp.

PAGE 34

"She's Acting Single, I'm Drinking Doubles"
Wayne Carson
Rose Bridge Music

"Jesus On The Radio, Daddy's On The Phone"
Tom T. Hall
Hallnote Music

"From The Bottle To The Bottom"
Kris Kristofferson
Combine Music Corp.

"Four In The Floor And A Fifth Beneath The Seat"
Finley Duncan, Jim Foster
Unart Music Corp. and Chu-Fin Music

"Whiskey"
Jerry Vann
Hallnote Music

PAGE 35

"The Bitter They Are, The Harder They Fall"
Larry Gatlin
First Generation Music Co.

PAGE 36

"If Practice Makes Perfect"
Larry Gatlin
First Generation Music Co.

"Low Down Ways"
Toy Caldwell
No Exit Music Co., Inc.

"She Even Woke Me Up To Say Goodbye"
Mickey Newbury, Douglas Gilmore
© 1969 Acuff-Rose Publications, Inc. Used by permission; all rights reserved

"Thank God and Greyhound"
Ed Nix, Larry Kingston
© 1970 Window Music Publishing Co., Inc.
Used by permission; all rights reserved

"Leavin' And Sayin' Goodbye"
Jeannie Seely
© 1971 Tree Publishing Co., Inc.

"When You Leave Amarillo, Turn Out The Lights"
Cindy Walker
Combine Music Corp.

PAGE 37

"She Just Loved The Cheatin' Out Of Me"
Sanger D. Shafer, A.L. "Doodle" Owens
© 1977 Acuff-Rose Publications, Inc.
Used by permission; all rights reserved

PAGE 38

"Why Have You Left The One You Left Me For?"
Bobby True
Mother Tongue Music

"Let's Say Goodbye Like We Said Hello (In A Friendly Kind Of Way)"
Ernest Tubb, Jimmy Skinner
Unichappell Music, Inc.

"(Lying Here With) Linda On My Mind"
Conway Twitty
© 1973 Twitty Bird Music Publishing Co.

"When I Stop Leaving I'll Be Gone"
Kent Robbins
Pi-Gem Music Publishers, Inc.

"I Don't Wanna Cry"
Larry Gatlin
First Generation Music Co.

PAGE 39

"She Don't Get Mad, She Just Gets Even"
Jerry K. Green
Con Brio Music

"Don't Tell Me You're Sorry"
Loretta Lynn
Sure Fire Music Co.

"We Lose A Little Ground"
Roy Baham
© New Keys Music, Inc.
Used by permission; all rights reserved

"You Can't Make A Heel Toe The Mark"
Ray Pennington
Tree Publishing Co., Inc.

"Pass Me By"
Hillman Hall
Hallnote Music

"I Don't Want To Play House"
Glenn Sutton, Billy Sherrill
Al Gallico Music Corp.

PAGE 40

"How Come My Dog Don't Bark"
Buck Owens
© 1977 Blue Book Music, Bakersfield, California

PAGE 41

"Fist City"
Loretta Lynn
Sure Fire Music Co.

"Don't Come Home A-Drinkin' With Lovin' On Your Mind"
Loretta Lynn, Peggy Wills
Sure Fire Music Co.

"You Can Have Her"
Bill Cook
Harvard Music Inc. and Big Billy Music

"Say 'Howdy Do' To Emmy-Lou's Ol' Man"
Kendal Franceschi
Concorde Publishing Co.

"Look What The Dog Drug In"
Joe Chambers
Galleon Music Inc. and Dudesong Music Inc.

"Say 'Howdy Do' To Emmy-Lou's Ol' Man"
Kendal Franceschi
Concorde Publishing Co.

"Let's Shake Hands And Come Out Lovin'"
Kenny O'Dell
Hungry Mountain Music

PAGE 42

"I Take A Lot Of Pride In What I Am"
Merle Haggard
Blue Book Music

"Coal Miner's Daughter"
Loretta Lynn
Sure Fire Music Co.

"My Heroes Have Always Been Cowboys"
Sharon Vaughn
Jack and Bill Music Co.

"I Got My Wife A Real Good Job"
Don King, Dave Woodward
Wiljex Publishing Co.

"The Older The Violin, The
  Sweeter The Music"
Claude Putnam
Tree Publishing Co., Inc.

"Genuine Texas Good
  Guy"
Dave Woodward and Jeff
  Walker
Wiljex Publishing Co.

PAGE 43

"If I'da Known I Was Gonna
  Live This Long"
Don King, Dave Woodward
Con Brio Music

PAGE 44

"The Undertaker's Gonna
  Have A Hard Time
  (Wipin' This Smile Offa
  My Face"
Sid Linard
Wiljex Publishing Co.

PAGE 45

"The Pop-A-Top Inn"
Don King, Dave Woodward
Wiljex Publishing Co.

"Please Don't Tell Me How
  The Story Ends"
Kris Kristofferson
Combine Music Corp.

"One Day At A Time"
Willie Nelson
© 1965 Tree Publishing Co.,
  Inc.

"Faster Horses"
Tom T. Hall
Hallnote Music

"Drop Kick Me Jesus"
Paul Craft
Black Sheep Music

"If I'da Known I Was Gonna
  Live This Long"
Don King, Dave Woodward
Con Brio Music

PAGE 46

"Proud To Keep It Country"
Don King, Dave Woodward
Wiljex Publishing Co.

ABOUT DOUG TODD

DOUG TODD is the public relations director of the Dallas Cowboys. He and some of his friends began writing down titles and lyrics of country and western songs several years ago. This is Todd's only hobby, as it's one of the few hobbies one can enjoy without having to stand up.

PENGUIN MODERN CLASSICS

THE FORTUNES OF RICHARD MAHONY

ULTIMA THULE

Ethel Florence Lindesay Richardson was born in Melbourne in 1870. Her Irish grandmother, a devotee of Handel, called her son Henry Handel and from him Richardson took her pen name.

Her father, Walter Lindesay Richardson, was born in Dublin and emigrated to Australia in the early 1850s. Her mother arrived at about the same time and Ethel was born fifteen years later. When she was three, she and her younger sister were taken to England, but while there her father learnt of the collapse of his financial affairs and returned to Australia.

Ethel Richardson spent an unhappy childhood, some of it at a select girls' boarding school, depicted by her in *The Getting of Wisdom* (1910). In 1888, nine years after her husband's death, Mrs Richardson took her daughters abroad so that Ethel could continue her musical studies in Leipzig. She spent most of the next sixteen years in Germany, where she met and married J. G. Robertson, later to become first Professor of German Literature at the University of London. In Leipzig, she experienced failure as a musician and turned to writing. Her first published novel was *Maurice Guest* (1908). Later, in England, she began *The Fortunes of Richard Mahony* (1917-1929), visiting Australia in 1912 to refresh her Australian memories. After her husband's death in 1933, she moved to Sussex, where she died in 1946.

HENRY HANDEL RICHARDSON

THE FORTUNES OF RICHARD MAHONY

Ultima Thule

With an Introduction by
LEONIE KRAMER

PENGUIN BOOKS

Penguin Books Ltd,
Harmondsworth, Middlesex, England
Penguin Books,
625 Madison Avenue, New York, N.Y. 10022, U.S.A.
Penguin Books Australia Ltd,
Ringwood, Victoria, 3134, Australia
Penguin Books Canada Ltd,
2801 John Street, Markham, Ontario, Canada
Penguin Books (N.Z.) Ltd,
182-190 Wairau Road, Auckland 10, New Zealand

First published by William Heinemann Limited 1929
Published in Penguin Books 1971
Reprinted 1976, 1978, 1980, 1981
Introduction copyright © Leonie Kramer, 1971

Made and printed in Hong Kong by
Wing Tai Cheung Printing Co. Ltd
Set in Linotype Times

Except in the United States of America,
this book is sold subject to the condition that
it shall not, by way of trade or otherwise, be lent,
re-sold, hired out, or otherwise circulated without
the publisher's prior consent in any form of
binding or cover other than that in which it is
published and without a similar condition
including this condition being imposed on the
subsequent purchaser.

CIP

Richardson, Henry Handel.
Ultima Thule.

(Penguin modern classics.)
Third volume in the author's trilogy: The fortunes
of Richard Mahony.
Previously published, Ringwood, Vic.: Penguin
Books, 1971; originally published, London:
William Heinemann, 1929.
ISBN 0 14 003339 4

I. Title: The fortunes of Richard
Mahony. (Series.)

A823'.2